D1709902

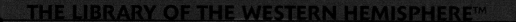

Exploring JAMAICA

with the FIVE Themes of Geography

by Jess Crespi

The Rosen Publishing Group's
PowerKids Press™
New York

Published in 2005 by The Rosen Publishing Group, Inc.
29 East 21st Street, New York, NY 10010

First Edition

Editor: Geeta Sobha
Book Design: Michelle Innes

Photo Credits: Cover, p. 1 © Bill Bachmann/Index Stock Imagery, Inc.; p. 9 © Gavin Wickham; Eye Ubiquitous/Corbis; pp. 9 (beach), 16 © Greg Johnston/Lonely Planet Images; p. 10 © Sergio Pitamitz/Corbis; p. 10 (butterfly) © Taylor S. Kennedy/National Geographic Image Collection; pp. 12, 15 (bauxite), 16 (Kingston) © Howard Davies/Corbis; p. 12 (Bob Marley) © Hulton Archive/Getty Images; p. 12 (cricket) © Gordon Brooks/AFP/Getty Images; pp. 15, 21 © Layne Kennedy/Corbis; p. 19 © David Cumming; Eye Ubiquitous/Corbis; p. 19 (ship) © Denis Anthony Valentine/Corbis

Library of Congress Cataloging-in-Publication Data

Crespi, Jess.
    Exploring Jamaica with the five themes of geography / by Jess Crespi.— 1st ed.
    p. cm. — (Library of the Western Hemisphere)
    Includes index.
    ISBN 1-4042-2674-5 (lib. bdg.) — ISBN 0-8239-4634-7 (pbk.)
    1. Jamaica—Geography—Juvenile literature. I. Title. II. Series.

F1874.5.C74 2005
917.29206—dc22

                                                                    2004000114

Manufactured in the United States of America

Contents

The FIVE Themes of Geography

Geography is the study of Earth, including its climate, resources, physical features, and people. To study a particular country or area, such as Jamaica, geographers use the five themes of geography: location, place, human-environment interaction, movement, and regions. These themes help us organize and understand important information about the geography of a country. Let's see what the five themes can tell us about the island of Jamaica.

1 Location

Where is Jamaica?

We can define where Jamaica is by using its absolute, or exact, location. Absolute location tells exactly where a place is in the world. The imaginary lines of longitude and latitude are used to find the absolute location of a place.

We can also define a place by using its relative, or general, location. Relative location tells where a place is in relation to other places nearby. Relative location can also be described by using cardinal directions: east, west, north, and south.

2 Place

What is Jamaica like?

By looking at Jamaica's physical and human features, we can get to know its land and its people. Physical features occur in nature. Landforms, bodies of water, climate, and plant and animal life are all examples of physical features. Human features are things, such as buildings, cities, and governments, that people have created.

3 Human-Environment Interaction

How do the people and the environment of Jamaica affect each other?

Human-environment interaction shows how the environment of Jamaica has affected the way Jamaicans live. Also, it explains how Jamaicans have adapted, or changed to fit, their environment.

4 Movement

How do people, goods, and ideas get from place to place in Jamaica?

Movement explains how products, people, and ideas move around Jamaica. It also shows how they move from Jamaica to other countries in the world.

5 Regions

What does Jamaica have in common with other places? How are places within Jamaica grouped?

Places are grouped into regions by similar features that they share. We will study features that Jamaica shares with other areas, making it part of a certain region. We'll also look at physical regions within Jamaica.

Jamaica is an island located in the Caribbean Sea. Its absolute location is 18° north and 77° west.

Jamaica's relative location can be determined by looking at the places that surround it. Jamaica is 90 miles (145 kilometers) south of the island of Cuba. It is 100 miles (161 km) west of the island of Hispaniola. The countries of Haiti and the Dominican Republic are located on the island of Hispaniola.

Where in the World?

Absolute location is the point where the lines of longitude and latitude meet.

Longitude tells a place's position in degrees east or west of the prime meridian, a line that runs through Greenwich, London.

Latitude tells a place's position in degrees north or south of the equator, the imaginary line that goes around the middle of the earth.

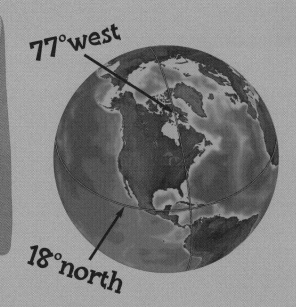

77° west

18° north

Kingston is Jamaica's capital and largest city. It is located on the southeastern coast of the country.

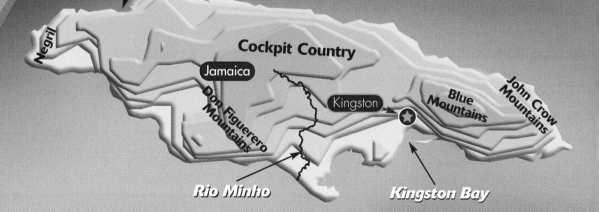

Montego Bay

Negril

Cockpit Country

Jamaica

Don Figuerero Mountains

Kingston

Blue Mountains

John Crow Mountains

Rio Minho

Kingston Bay

Caribbean Sea

Physical Features

Jamaica is the third largest island in the Caribbean Sea. Like the other Caribbean islands, Jamaica is actually formed by underwater mountain chains. Most of the land of Jamaica is mountains and hills. There are plains on the southern coast. The land along the coast is flat, with miles of white, sandy beaches. Karst, or limestone, hills and plateaus lie in the western part of the island. This area is called Cockpit Country. Deep caves and gorges can also be found there. The Rio Minho, in central Jamaica, is the longest river in the country.

Because it is so close to the equator, Jamaica has a tropical climate. The temperature stays around 80° F (27° C) almost everywhere in the country. The rainy season is from September to November. The country faces severe hurricanes during the late summer and fall.

Jamaica is famous for its beautiful beaches. This one is located on the coast of the city of Negril in the west.

The Blue Mountains, in the east, are the highest parts of Jamaica.

Dunn's River Falls is made up of 600 feet (183 meters) of waterfalls.

Jamaica's giant swallowtail is the largest butterfly in the Western Hemisphere.

High in the mountains, small trees grow. Rain forests are found in the valleys. About one-quarter of the 3,000 types of plants that grow on the island can only be found in Jamaica. Cedar, pimento, coconut, and ebony are some of the trees that grow in Jamaica.

Parrots, cuckoos, and hummingbirds are a few of the 28 types of birds found in Jamaica. Bats, the Jamaican boa, and turtles inhabit this island. The American crocodile lives in the streams and rivers. The West Indian manatee can be found in Jamaica's coastal waters.

Human Features

About 2,700,000 people live on the island of Jamaica. One-third of them live in Jamaica's capital city, Kingston. Jamaica's national motto is "Out of many, one people." Jamaica is truly a mixture of

Bob Marley was Jamaica's most famous reggae musician.

Cricket is Jamaica's national sport. Many Jamaican players are members of the West Indies cricket team.

Spanish Town was Jamaica's capital from 1692 to 1872.

many cultures. The styles of buildings in Spanish Town, in the south, are evidence of Jamaica's first European settlers from Spain. British influence can be found in many customs, including sports such as soccer and cricket. English is the official language of Jamaica, although Jamaicans mostly speak their own form of English called creole. African influence can be found in the popular Jamaican style of music called reggae. Most Jamaicans are descended from Africans. Other Jamaicans are descended from peoples from India, China, and Germany.

Jamaica's form of government is called a parliamentary democracy. Although the queen of England is still the head of state, Jamaica became an independent country in 1962. The government is led by Jamaica's prime minister.

Jamaicans live in all parts of the country, even in the mountainous areas, such as the rough land of Cockpit Country. However, most Jamaicans live in coastal urban areas, such as Kingston, Savanna la Mar, and Montego Bay.

Jamaicans rely on the natural resources of their country. The land itself is a resource for farmers. Farming and raising livestock are important parts of Jamaica's economy. Although only about 20 percent of the land is good for farming, Jamaican farmers grow a wide variety of fruits, plants, and vegetables. Sugar is the most important crop.

Minerals, such as salt and lead, are natural resources that are important to Jamaica's economy. Jamaicans mine many different minerals in the mountain regions. The most important mineral is bauxite. Jamaica is one of the largest bauxite producers in the world.

Bauxite contains aluminum, which is used in manufacturing products such as cars.

Farmers grow coffee plants in the Blue Mountains of Jamaica.

Air pollution in Kingston affects the environment as well as the health of the people living there.

Pesticides used by farmers drain into coastal waters, affecting the coral reefs.

Over the past century, Jamaica's industries have grown. At times this growth has negatively affected Jamaica's environment. Jamaican wood, such as mahogany, has been sold around the world for building cabinets and furniture. However, cutting down these trees has destroyed much of Jamaica's forests.

Cities such as Kingston are faced with air pollution due to automobile traffic. Wastes from factories have polluted waterways. Even the beautiful coral reefs are in danger due to oil spills and polluted water.

In 2001, the National Environment and Planning Agency (NEPA) was set up to help protect Jamaica's natural resources. Groups such as the Jamaica Environment Trust work hard to educate people about environmental concerns. Animals such as the coney and the manatee are being protected by law to avoid extinction.

4 Movement

Moving around Jamaica can be difficult. Most people do not own cars. There are many taxis in the cities, but they are very expensive, and most people can't afford to use them. Brightly colored buses offer most Jamaicans an affordable form of transportation. Goods are shipped in and out of Jamaica through ports such as Kingston, Ocho Rios, Rocky Point, and Montego Bay. Although Jamaica is small, it has about 35 airports to accommodate people and goods moving in and out of the country. The two main airports are the Norman W. Manley International Airport in Kingston and the Donald Sangster Airport in Montego Bay.

There are about eight television stations and over 25 radio stations that provide news and entertainment. These radio and television stations also exchange information with stations in other Caribbean countries.

Kingston is the main port in Jamaica for both shipping and cruise ships.

Jamaicans depend on buses to move them from place to place.

19

Jamaica is part of a geographical region known as the West Indies. The West Indies is a group of islands in the Caribbean Sea. They stretch from the south of Florida to the northern coast of South America.

Physical regions within Jamaica are the coastal plains, the karst limestone hills of Cockpit Country, and the mountainous areas that make up most of the country. Mountain regions within Jamaica include the Don Figuerero Mountains in the south and the John Crow Mountains in the east.

The country is divided into three counties—Cornwall, Middlesex, and Surrey. The counties are divided into smaller areas called parishes.

Jamaica is also part of the Commonwealth of Nations. This group is made up of countries that were once ruled by England. Canada, Australia, South Africa, and India are also members.

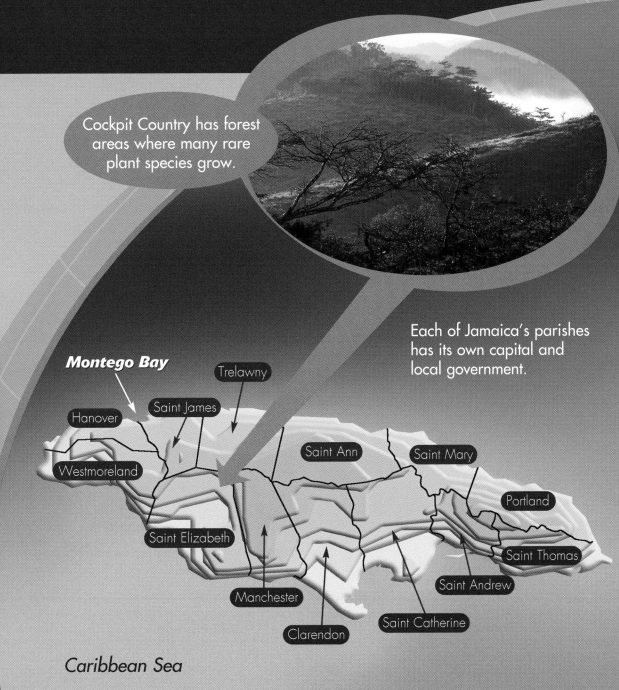

Cockpit Country has forest areas where many rare plant species grow.

Each of Jamaica's parishes has its own capital and local government.

Montego Bay

Trelawny

Hanover

Saint James

Westmoreland

Saint Ann

Saint Mary

Portland

Saint Elizabeth

Saint Thomas

Manchester

Saint Andrew

Clarendon

Saint Catherine

Caribbean Sea

Jamaica's Flag

FACT ZONE

Population (2003) 2,695,867

Language English

Absolute location 18° north, 77° west

Capital city Kingston

Area 4,244 square miles (10,991 square kilometers)

Highest point Blue Mountain Peak 7,401 feet (2,256 meters)

Lowest point Caribbean Sea zero feet

Land boundaries none

Natural resources bauxite, gypsum, and limestone

Agricultural products sugarcane, bananas, coffee, potatoes, vegetables, poultry, goats, and milk

Major exports aluminum, bauxite, sugar, bananas, and rum

Major imports machinery and transportation equipment, construction materials, fuel, food, chemicals, and fertilizers

Glossary

architecture (AR-ki-tek-chur) The style in which buildings are designed.

bauxite (bok-SYT) A rock that contains aluminum.

coral reef (KOR-uhl REEF) Rock made up of sea animals called polyps.

creole (KREE-ohl) A spoken language that comes from another main language, such as English.

culture (KUHL-chur) The way of life, ideas, customs, and traditions shared by a group of people.

descended (di-SEND-ud) To belong to a later generation of the same family.

extinction (ek-STINGKT-shuhn) When something no longer exists.

gorge (GORJ) A valley that has steep, rocky sides.

interaction (in-tur-AK-shuhn) The action between people, groups, or things.

limestone (LIME-stohn) A rock formed from the remains of shells or coral.

region (REE-juhn) An area or a district.

resource (ri-SORSS) Something that is valuable or useful to a place or person.

Index

A
air pollution, 17
American crocodile, 11

B
bauxite, 14
beaches, 8

C
Caribbean Sea, 6, 8, 20
Cockpit Country, 8, 14, 20
Commonwealth of Nations, 20
coral reefs, 17
counties, 20
creole, 13
cricket, 13

E
environment, 17
extinction, 17

F
farming, 14

G
gorges, 8

H
hurricanes, 8

I
industries, 17

J
Jamaica Environment Trust, 17

K
Kingston, 11, 14, 17, 18

P
parishes, 20
parliamentary democracy, 13

R
rain forests, 11
reggae, 13
resources, 14, 17
Rio Minho, 8
river, 8, 11

S
soccer, 13
Spain, 13
Spanish Town, 13

W
West Indian manatee, 11, 17
West Indies, 20

Web Sites

Due to the changing nature of Internet links, PowerKids Press has developed an on-line list of Web sites related to the subject of this book. This site is updated regularly. Please use this link to access the list:
http://www.powerkidslinks.com/lwh/jamaica